Wave

To Ian —
with thanks for all your
encouragement & support
Bests Pat Jan '08

Pat Borthwick

Templar Poetry

First published 2007 by Templar Poetry
Templar Poetry is an imprint of Delamide & Bell

Fenelon House,
Kingsbridge Terrace
Dale Road, Matlock, Derbyshire
DE4 3NB

www.templarpoetry.co.uk

ISBN 978-1-906285-01-2

Typeset by Pliny
Graphics by Paloma Violet
Printed and bound in India

To my special friends, Ian and Mike

Acknowledgements

'Visit', 1st Prize Torriano Open 2007 and Brittle Star 2007: 'A Son', 1st Prize Norwich Open 2007 and Outbox and Other Poems Anthology (Leaf Books 2007): 'Passing On the Tickle', 1st Prize Silver Wyvern, Poetry on the Lake, Italy 2006: 'Snow', Bedford Square (John Murray 2006): 'In the Consulting Room', 2nd Prize Anglo-Canadian Petra Kenney 2006: 'The Man Who Collected Teapots', Ilkley Literature Festival 2006, HC and Newark Open 2007, HC: 'Bought Cakes', 2nd Prize Long Poems, Scintilla 9 and Bedford Square (John Murray 2006) and Swim (Mudfog 2005): 'Murder', 2nd Prize Frogmore 2005 and Bedford Square (John Murray 2006) and Swim (Mudfog 2005): 'Visiting Father...', Seam 2006 and Bedford Square (John Murray 2006) and Swim (Mudfog 2005), 'Beech House', 1st Prize Woldswords Open 2005 and Lancaster Lit Fest Anthology 2005 and Swim (Mudfog 2005): 'Katya', 1st Prize Amnesty International Human Rights 2005 and Swim (Mudfog 2005): 'Grass', 2nd Prize Torriano Open 2006: 'A Reasonable Question...', Ver Open 2007, HC.

My thanks go to The Arvon Foundation, Madingley, Ty Newydd, The Poetry School, The Poetry Business, Aldeburgh and Beverley Festivals and Chris North at Almassera, Spain, for their inspiring programmes of gutsy courses and workshops.

And to the generosity and encouragement from other poet friends.

Contents

Visit

Had I known you were there
I would have knocked softly
or slipped off my shoes.

I watch your wings open and close
like hands
uncertain of prayer,

your plumed antennae
write manuscripts
around the whitewashed walls.

Then alter them.
Then alter them again
as you explore the realm of my laptop

finding it to be part of a table
and the table part of a floor, a room,
a whole city, a planet. A single point.

O mighty little thing I cannot name,
the Moon must have spooned you in
between the tides of my curtains.

Until I Did

I never understood
why my brother,
at the bottom of his wardrobe
underneath his Table Tennis Weeklies,
kept a pile of magazines
filled with slouching orange ladies.
Of course, I could never ask,
but I knew
how being curious about the world
was meant to be good.

I never understood
why in the top drawer of their dressing table,
under Father's laundered handkerchiefs
with their embroidered monograms,
were these strange shapes
like cut off fingers from an industrial glove.
Out of curiosity
(and if he'd stand still long enough)
I used to put one on the dog's docked tail
then watch him wag it off.

There were many other things
I didn't understand
until one day, I did.

A Son

You'd have been a young man now,
even your imperfections perfect. I've seen you
dipping under arches down the Cam,
your tall reflection among upturned fiery trees

and not a single drip from your quant pole.
At ten, you taught yourself to cook Thai;
simple blossoms in red-glazed vases
set to the exact geographic East of our plates.

Do you remember when you were six,
how you poured warm oil in a tjanting
then showed me how to bathe Toby's eyes
before he trundled into hibernation?

From your pram you could hollow a pumpkin
and carve any expression in it.
The candle's amber flame
chuckled on the gatepost all night. Blackberries.

Our hands are still stained and clotted. That too
was in October. You are especially in October,
October the twenty-eighth, a Thursday,
the day I had to use my overnight case.

Can we get you anything? the nurses asked,
with their eyes hidden in their pockets.

Passing On the Tickle

Lie flat as sky, sleeves rolled to the elbow
so that, arms outstretched, your hands

hinge through the grassy overhang
to where water runs in shadows

and hollow reeds set notes free.
All possibilities are in this place.

It's here the speckled trout waits
gleaming in war-flecked armour.

For now, he's made himself invisible.
But you saw his flash of leap and catch,

his muddy swirl and dash.
And you know he faces upstream

breathing in, breathing out. And close -
his contemplation, the next plump fly

or next, the deliciousness of this one
snatched from heaven's bright mouth.

You were taught to watercreep your fingers
towards where he wafts his fins.

Are you closer to pectoral or pelvic,
the narrowing of sword to tail?

A clash of artistry. His argent muscle
tightens to attention as you make touch.

D-rum, d-rum, d-rumdiddy d-rum. He feels
your drowning beat. *D-rumdiddy d-rum*. Hook

two fingers in his closing gill and he's in air.
Your father, grandfather, his father, his,

throng the grassy bank, caps doffed.
Well done lad, well done. You watch

their hungry plates and cutlery
zig-zag to the bottom of the stream

while about to break your family line,
return him to his water. *D-rumdiddy d-rum*.

Snow

Snow began quietly, like we did.
And then I heard you everywhere.

Up the path, footprints
I'm not exactly proud of.

No doubt it was a long walk
from your car to my door.

For years I promised myself
I'd never let this happen again.

Here it is though, and here's me,
sure of every reason why it should.

Now you've stepped into my life
and when the thaw comes

we both know these tracks
will stay and you will be hurt.

I will be hurt. She will be hurt.
Outside, a sudden blackcap

lands in the centre of my mahonia.
It's found the flower spike

and is stripping petals one by one.
Look my darling, more snow

and the windows drifting.
Corners, edges, under blown white.

In The Consulting Room

Do sit down, he says,
pointing to the jolly-coloured chair
perhaps assuming
they'll sit on each other's knees.
He picks up the phone,
requests another be brought in.

They're joined at the sternum,
have shared the same blouses
and stretchy cardigans, heart,
for twenty years.
Their memories and imaginations
have been visited by the same blood. At night,
they pass the same breath between them.
It wreathes their dreams.
Sometimes, their lips rest on each other's.

So how have you been? Any problems
since I last saw you?

nono, they reply,
pulling at their knitted cuffs.

Stairs still manageable? Sleep well?
yesyes

Eating? Any difficulty there? Bowels?

nono

They reach for a mint
from each other's pocket.

A clinical sister brings in an x-ray,
fixes it against the light box.
And leaves.
They both turn their heads,
see a pattern of pale bones
like snowy branches,
timber from a ghost ship.
They see a huge dark shape
hung from the spars,
a pulsar, an exploding star.

So, have you thought about
what we talked about last time,
reached a decision?

Sweet wrappers spill from their laps.

yesyes. nono. yesno.

The Man Who Collected Teapots

I knew a man who collected teapots.
Some he paid a lot for, others

he'd spotted lidless at a car boot or
the back of a cupboard in the village hall.

So much history brewed in teapots, he said,
pouring me a cup from Samian ware,

its little sprigged figures chasing each other
round a red glazed almond tree.

He taught himself Japanese joinery
so he could make shelves with secret joints.

Think teapots, he said arranging them,
think love of craft, the craft of love. He told me

that to make a teapot, an apprentice
needed to master seven skills, how

the lid must fit with the sound
a good decision makes, the pulling

of a left handle being more complex
than a right, how the potter's

thumbprints remained for his children
to outgrow. *The throw lines on the spout*

must follow the rotation of the Earth
if you want to pour clean and well.

He filled his high shelves in the alcoves
and across the chimney breast: the order

and angle of each pot, exactly considered.
Then he set out every chair he could find,

turned them to face the teapots, and although
the whole village had invitations, no one came.

Except a wren who flew through the open door,
searching for somewhere safe to build a nest.

Bought Cakes

I

Staring us in the face it was. What
else, with the wagons on the verge
refusing to come up our drive?
March was different,
coming for the ewes.
We were all green then.
Some in lamb
and all them little wet-lambs.
Can't fault the men. I
stayed in the house with Jen,
managed to pull a curtain off its track.
First row we'd had in thirty years
and some game show on the telly,
two families, all teeth
and clapping when they lost.

II

That night in bed,
between long case chimes,
Jen thought she heard a bleat
coming from the orchard. Looking
down we made out one they
must have missed,
a hungry half-day ghost running
round and round the damsons.
I had to dig it deep,
and the flint I used to tap it.
Our bed seemed smaller after that.

III

And then again, two months on,
the feed bins almost empty
and us ready for new Point of Lays.
Despite all our careful phone calls
the transport refused driving through the gates
to take the old girls. Government instructions.
But no one thought to mention them to us.
We'd two thousand would flow into the field
when Sally barked to wake the cock
and Jen rolled up their metal doors.
Like a tidal wave, all combs and clucks
and feathers and Sally somewhere in there.
You could set the clock by it. Then breakfast.

IV

So, as I said, staring me in the face it was. What else?
I'd have to neck them each by hand, starting after dark.
Jason, just back from university, said I spoke too
soft to hear, and was his boiler suit still hung
behind the door? Eleven-hour shifts we worked,
with one hour off, not stopping till three days on
we saw it done. Our hands were raw, our wrists
and arms and backs in a rhythm that let in pain
once it slowed. Jen had to hold the mug to my mouth,
cut up my food, undo my fly and that.

V

Not too long before the stench wormed
from the shed and under all our doors.
Jace on the tractor, Sally on the trailer with him,
Jen, fetching empty paper sacks and rags, me wood,
then down for that drum of sump behind the bales
to cart up to top field. Toppers Feld. Slow.
First time in the lamb barn since.

VI

One match.

VII

Two days before we saw the sky empty of feather ash.
Before that circle cooled. And Sally still not back.

VIII

Jace and I, we don't know what to do.
She's hidden it in the filing cabinet bottom drawer.
Memento Mori. Must be Sal's. It's in an ice-cream box.
Just fits, nose to back of skull. She found it
raking through before we got the digger in.
Won't bury it, like she has her tongue. Gone mute,
won't even wind the clocks or put the kettle on.

IX

Jason's back there and sitting finals now.
The television spills across our knees.
The choice is war, or games
where people wave and laugh a lot.
I read they've unearthed tortoise shells
carved with what might be words,
or attempts at words, from 8,000 years ago,
that today, three-quarters questioned
didn't know the time it took to soft-boil eggs.
That curtain still needs fixing.
We're managing just fine. Getting by.

X

Will that do? Never did like cameras.
Can you turn it off now? An arts programme?
I'm sorry they were only bought cakes.

Murder

Late on my seventh birthday
my brother murdered somebody
and was asking me, in my pyjamas,
to share and keep his deadly secret.

That night we sat on hessian sacks
in our shadowy allotment shed.
Moonlight slid its tongue
across fork tines and spade shanks.

Upturned terra cotta pots
towered on the prick-out bench.
Oil cans occasionally gave off
a metal burp scattering the crawlies.

Still sticky with warm blood
his hands reach for mine,
press something hush-hush
and squelchy-squishy in them.

Eye sockets, he says. *Don't look.*
Let your fingers feel inside.
Eyeballs, he says, swapping them
for something squeezable, moist

but twice as cold. *Teeth. The tongue.*
Piece by piece I hold his slimy crime
and promise a sister's silence.
Then a dumb stump of head.

I know its dome of veinwork, chin,
its wrinkles, cheekbones, twisted nerves.
I know it is our father's. And I know why.
Until the plank door bangs open and

on the jamb hangs his beery profile.
His torch prances across a slatted box
stacked with cut tomatoes, Brussels sprouts,
ten peeled carrots, two kiwis, one courgette,

my brother's hands sparkling with ketchup.

Visiting Father in the Side Room off the Geriatric Ward and Reading the Notice Above His Sink.

Wet hands thoroughly.
Apply liquid stop.
Rub palm to charm.
Fright palm first over left dorsum.
Then left alarm over fighting force dumb.
Harm to harm, fingers in too haste.
Racks of stingers to opposing swarms,
lingus interlocked.
Rotational rubbing of right thumb
clasped in deft spurt
and vice reverse.
Raw painful shoving back and forwards
with clasped lingers of might hand.
In left spawn and twice measure
and worse.
Rinse and withdraw hands.
Apply one pleasure of alcohol rub
using the midweek prescribed
for 10-15 year olds. Remember
to keep nails abort and unseen.
Don't forget
to apply for reconditioning cream.
Don't forget
To leave your gown and loves in the bin
And to keep the door closed.
Wash hands. Wash hands. Wash hands.

Steps

and more numerous.

are steeper, slower

and cleaned twice a day)

in a nice shade of rose

(though carpeted

the stairs to your room

Each time I visit,

Beech House

The older folk keep to their beds,
their wings tied with muslin.
Through his netted window
my uncle is content to see the moon
open its bright eye. Or is that the sun?
A single snowflake?
Strange, how the snow is so accurate.
Year by year, in a sort of symmetry
it finds and fills his window, only his,
whichever street he's living in.
His grandchildren's children
have built snowmen in the garden
like last month's, and down the corridor
where wheelchairs and zimmers
are parked for the night.
Some have been abandoned,
their owners gone missing.
They'll not get away with it.
Up on the poop deck -
a row of uniforms with telescopes.
They'll sort it out. On his single shelf
there's a biscuit and a meteorite.
And a ship in a bottle painted with stars.
In the bedside drawer, he keeps the Queen

and his medal. And his house keys because
he's *not staying long. Go away,* he shouts,
as they try to untie his bib. *Go away.*
All hands. Up hammocks. Bring my quadrant.
Dead reckoning time. He's bent at the window.
Newton, Copernicus, Einstein, Herschel,
Aristoteles, Hercules, Julius Caesar,
Billy, Hell, Beer, Parrot, Short, Airy. There!
That's where we landed, he says, pointing
to the Moon, the Sun, a snowflake.
Still naming craters. *Such magnificent desolation.*
Outside, the beech trees applaud fidgety stars
and the man at the window counting.
Do you know our module only has one ascent engine?
There is never a second chance?

The Collectors

I wonder if Mr and Mrs Martin Ryerson
have the key ring and mouse mat,
the tea towel and sketchbook
with the same Monet on them
as the one in their private collection
in the basement vault?
Houses of Parliament, London. Circa 1900.
Such pretty pastels.
Perhaps it's on Mrs Ryerson's spongeable apron,
the one she's wearing now
to prepare tea for Martin who, incidentally,
is cutting the lawn.
Tiny stars of grass whirl up
and are caught in the box
on the front of his mower -
that's a new line from the gallery shop
aimed at men.
See how vibrations from the motor
make pink and blue clouds
scuddle round Big Ben.
You can almost hear it judder and chime.
Is that why Mrs Ryerson dropped a mug
and her apron wrinkled momentarily
as if the Thames were on a rip tide,

all the tourist boats making for the quay
where today's tourists queue for the London Eye?
They want the real thing,
not an oily truth that shifts.
Mr Ryerson, ready for his tea,
will be disappointed. His picture,
in china smithereens, across the parquet floor.
He knows it so well now
and feels sure that splash of raw sienna
in the bottom right hand corner
must have been where Monet spilt his demi-tasse.
Or something stronger. On everything he's seen
that orange comes out a different shade. Isn't that
exactly what Monet was striving to achieve?

In Praise of the Oologists' Art

You have to admire their patience;
long before night-vision binoculars,
a pin-point focus shaded by two hands.
All that waiting through crepuscular light
as Spring turns leaves blood-red then gold.

A man from Cleethorpes adapted his ladder
by adding a metal crosier head to each rail
so having reached a sturdy lower branch
he could stretch and hook a higher one
then climb again, dittoing upwards. Simply

genius, but of course, he could never patent it
and soon all eggers had their own.
His innovation spread on winged whispers.
And such beautiful primed bodies secreted
under thermal layers and down-filled anoraks.

Hours spent on press-ups, pounding lanes.
How else to clamber down a cliff face
or scale a crag, inch up a swaying tree-top
with one hand left free? Such dexterity
to lift the clutch into a straw-lined tin.

It takes thirteen years to perfect this art; seven
for 'Recognition' from the house sparrow
to rarity; how greenish eggs are from a tree,
the speckled ones, a bush or near the ground;
learn to drill a tiny hole, cut sacs with a scalpel.

Or the fastidiousness of catalogue, columns,
a quill pen dipped in black ink to scribe
an A.O.U. Species Number on each shell.
Another six more years they say
to perfect these individual stages.

Then the apogee - new osprey eggs
swaddled in cotton wool, arranged
in narrow drawers with a cedar sawdust bed.
This last, the way a midwife lowers a stillborn
into its mother's arms. As expert as that.

Katya

Not of my own choosing
do my paps darken like muzzles.
My belly slowly swells.
I cannot see my valley now.
I crave for lassi
but they bring us rusty water
in the bottom of a can.

They come and come,
day, night, day,
unbuttoning
as the door slaps against the stucco.
They leave our thighs and faces
crusty with their stink.

And after me,
they hump across on to my mother,
covering her shrunken face
with her heavy dirndl skirt.
She is dry, dry.
Her womb is a husk.

Each day I am ripening.
I do not want this cuckoo
fluttering its rabid wings
in my darkness.
I can see its wild eyes beneath my skin.
It will suck me dry as rock.

Yet, I have practised its birth -
how I will keep my legs far apart,
my eyes screwed shut,
then roll it with my heel in the dust
kicking it and its afterbirth
down the mountainside.

Or, how I will say, *Give me my baby,*
and boy or girl, call it Katya.
That was my mother's name.

Grass

(Surely the people is grass. Is XI 7)

Gather a root of grass
from every lawn in the world,
every sports pitch and gutter,
barrack and hospital ground,
fold yard and pasture, watery bank,
concrete crevice and crack,
wherever grass might force through
to wave its green flags.

And look under things
like wagons shunted away
down the branch line, a churn,
rusting headstocks, long-handled tools,
the soles of the man left waiting.
Yellow it might be
but grass knows how to survive.
It never complicates air.
It travels the world
by linking arms with its neighbour.

With these roots, start a new lawn
in a place where everyone
can walk barefoot across it

(at least once in their lives) to feel
how something as simple as grass
knows how to sing so flutey and free
you need to get down on your knees
and tune your ear to its frequency.
O grass, what have we made you hear?

And after we named you 'grass'
then renamed you 5^1(TTTAGGG) n-3^1,
what words did the wind bring
to make you cower and tremble?

Nimble Will, Squirrel Tail, Tumble and Quitch,
Quaking Grass, Ribbon Grass, Velvet and Witch,
Bristle, Spear, Panic, Redtop and Switch,
why have we made you brandish your swords?

What do you know?

A Reasonable Question for a Poet to Ask the Visiting Speaker on Optics at the Astronomical Society Meeting.

When I look through my telescope,
spiral galaxies and comets, planets,
things I cannot see, slide down the tube
and, through the black hole in my iris, enter me.

Then my heart beats from the edge of the Universe
so loud, stars are set quaking in my bright dark.
Even Taurus shies behind my breastbone,
thinking he hears a stampede. So why,

when I step aside from my tripod and gaze up
are all the stars back in their place,
the exact multitude and brightness as before -
while they still inhabit me?